I0503674

CONTENTS

Title Page

Book Goal

Who is This Book For?

What's in This Book?

Are You Working with a Good Product/Service?

PART 1 - General Sales Guidelines   1

Sales is a Process   2

It Bears Repeating: The Relationship is the   4
Most Important Part of the Process

In Other Words, Don't Be a Dick   6

Get to Know People   8

Don't Puke All Over a Meal That Has Been   10
Served to You on a Platter

Establish Good Habits Early   12

Adapting   14

Read More   16

Business Meals   18

Let's Party   20

Put Your Phone Down   22

Perception of Others' Work Gets in The Way of Actual Work and Creates Stress   24

Find The Loophole   27

How to Say "Hey Douchebag, I Need You to do Your Job" Nicely   30

Problem Solving   33

Truth and Action Work Best   34

Speak The Truth in Short Simple Sentences   36

Throw Out "The Sales Alphabet"   39

Avoiding Travel Burnout   41

Retain Your Clients   43

PART 2 - Starting a New Sales Job/Sales Endeavor   45

Starting in Sales   46

Training for The Job   48

What is the Value of The Product?   50

Who Will Get Shit Done Here For Me?   53

What Non-People Resources Are Available for Me to do My Job?   56

What Are Current Clients' Success Stories?   58

What's Needed to Deliver The Product or Service to The Client?   60

Where are The Pain Points the Product or Service Solves?   63

Organization is KEY   68

Identifying Targets   70

Identify the Title(s) of The People Who Make   72
the Buying Decision

Associations   74

Build Relationships with The Association's   77
Employees

Collecting Contact Information   79

The Email Trick   81

Reaching Out to The Right People - Get   82
Attention

Reaching Out to a New Client You Have Little   84
to No Information About

Playing "The New Person Card"   87

Reaching Out to a Client Who You Have   89
Detailed Information About

Priority Scale Ratings   92

What to Do if No One Responds   95

How to Respond When They Do Respond   98

The Initial Phone Call   101

Goals of an initial phone call   104

How to Get a Meeting   107

Traveling Without Confirmed Meetings   110

How to Handle Conferences   112

Meeting in Person: Listen More, Talk Less   116

Ask Your Question. Then Shut the Fuck Up. 120

Ask a Few Personal Questions 123

Mimicry: Be a Parrot 125

The Post-Meeting Follow Up 128

Maintaining Relationships 130

More on That: Being an Annoying Sales Person vs. a Good Sales Person 132

Keep Following Up: Making Warm Relationships Warmer 135

Developing the Relationship Through Meals and Entertainment 138

General Timelines for Following Up 141

Respond as fast as possible 144

Getting Closer to The Actual Sale 146

When They're Going to Buy From You 148

Bringing in The Money 151

A Completed Sale 153

Getting Credit: Perception is Reality 155

Vacation Planning 157

Building and Expanding Your Portfolio 159

Freeing up Your Future Time After You Have an Established Portfolio 161

This is the End of the Book 163

HOW TO BE SUCCESSFUL IN SALES STARTING ON DAY ONE

by

Pat Treuer

BOOK GOAL

I was in corporate sales working for Fortune 100 companies for 12 years. I traveled the world, experienced and learned, and by the end of that chapter of my life was able to walk away from the corporate world to pursue my own dreams. The lessons from this book are designed to help you achieve the same financial success – sooner than I did.

During my time in sales, I made too many mistakes to count. I learned from most of them. I hope to pass these lessons along to you, so you can avoid making those mistakes yourself and achieve success more quickly. Most ideas and guidelines in this book are a result of my mistakes, as well as general observations and lessons that were given to me. I don't claim any of these are original. In fact, if you notice any that correlate to an actual study or research, let me know so I can do a second edition that includes these "fun facts".

I hope you happily achieve success (however you define it) and can pursue what you want to. For me, that's making people laugh. That's a part of what I want to do here, as well as pass along the incredible breath of information, tactics/strategies, and processes I learned from my time in sales. I am still learning as I have started my own businesses and am currently following these the same guidelines and processes outlined in this book.

The first book in this series, *Considering a Career in Sales and How to Get The Job You Want,* covered getting a sales job. This one covers starting that job out. Here's an outline of how to succeed in sales to make money, save time, and define your own path, beginning on Day One. My goal with this book is to help one person. If any part helps you, please reach out and let me know. My contact information is at the end.

WHO IS THIS BOOK FOR?

This book is for anyone starting in sales or looking to improve their sales skills. You could be in an entry level sales job, or an entrepreneur who started your own business and have never done sales before. Or you may have worked in sales for some time and are looking for some new approaches.

The steps in this book require a lot of work up front, so you can be in cruise control later and dedicate your energy to what you really want in life, or to figuring out what that is.

WHAT'S IN THIS BOOK?

Part 1 of this book lays out the general guidelines of sales for you to keep in mind when starting out, so you can maintain your sanity and design processes to create your own success. Part 2 contains step by step instructions for starting a sales job or beginning a new sales endeavor.

The order in which you read these two parts is up to you. The general ideas in Part 1 are a good foundation, but you may want to get right to the step by step "how to" portion of the book, Part 2.

Again, this is Book 2 of my series on sales. I do refer to the other books as reference points, and that is because I want to keep things as simple and concise as possible. I believe there are three levels of sales. Level One is thinking about sales, covered in the first book, *Considering a Career in Sales and How To Get The Job You Want.* Level two is starting in sales (this book). Level three is advanced sales (book 3 of the series).

Before you read either part of this book, determine if you are selling a good product or service that creates value and is reliable. If it not, you need to find something else. The following chapter covers how to determine if it is worthwhile or not.

ARE YOU WORKING WITH A GOOD PRODUCT/ SERVICE?

You need to answer this question before starting in sales. There are countless examples of both good and bad products and services to work with. The following are a few very simple ways of identifying them. If you want more detail, you can find relevant chapters in Book 1.

These are by no means all encompassing.

- If the company measures your performance by how many phone calls or emails you are sending vs. actual results, it is most likely a garbage product or service.

- If the company has positive client reviews on their website, (yes, these are selected by the company) that tends to indicate a good product or service.

- If you notice the product or service in your everyday life, it is probably a good product.

Something else to consider: find out if the product is something people rely on or enjoy. People are lazy and want to do what is easiest for them and makes their own jobs easier. When you're selling a product that will make someone else's life or tasks easier, you are off to a good start. That product can almost sell itself. If you are selling something that isn't enjoyable and doesn't make things easier or more effective, you don't want that job.

PART 1 - GENERAL SALES GUIDELINES

SALES IS A PROCESS

This book is for medium to long term cycle sales. Some elements of the book can help with short term sales (meaning the client is likely to buy on first interaction with the sales person, as in retail sales).

Medium and long term sales, for sake of this book, are considered sales that take longer than 3 months to complete from the first interaction with a potential client. These are sales that affect your clients' direct business, meaning they will put thought and effort into making sure they select a good provider. You can't take the short term sales mentality into a medium or long term sales strategy or interaction with your potential clients. This will scare them off.

Your goals at each step of this process are as follows:

1. Identify potential clients.
2. Get an in-person meeting with them.
3. Develop a **relationship** with them.
4. Get them to buy what you are selling.

That relationship in Step 3 is key. Without this, there is no sale.

Many people will go into the first meeting placing the immediate sale of the product or service ahead of developing a relationship with the person. This is a common mistake, and a great way to piss potential clients off.

You want to build trust with these people. This is established through multiple interactions. The way to get these is to focus on building a positive relationship with a person up front, so they want to continue interacting with you. They won't want to interact with you again if you lead with trying to sell them something. When trust is established, people will start to think that buying from you is their idea instead of yours which will ultimately win you the business.

IT BEARS REPEATING: THE RELATIONSHIP IS THE MOST IMPORTANT PART OF THE PROCESS

People work with people they like. People work with people they trust. People develop trust through conversation and spending time with people. Get a person to like you and they will want to spend time with you.

Get them to spend time with you and they will feel invested in you. Get them to feel invested in you – and prove you're invested in them – and they will start to trust you. Get them to trust you and you will be able to sell them your product/service and possibly make a new friend.

During your first interactions with people, your focus needs to be on getting them to like you and see a professional reason to interact with you. Remember that. The how-to part of developing a relationship is addressed in part 2. The relationship is the most important part of this whole process.

IN OTHER WORDS, DON'T BE A DICK

T he converse of people working with people they like is that they only work with people they don't like when they are forced to. When starting out, focus on being as nice as possible to everyone you may encounter. Make it so people associate your name with positive feelings.

If you are friendly, smile, and work hard, all while showing you're competent, you'll see the following results with people you will work with:

- **Clients:** You will win more business. They will choose to work with you because they like you and they will recommend other people to work with you as well. Being liked when you have something decent or better to sell is the underlying foundation of sales.

- **Bosses/Senior Leadership:** Believe it or not, people get promoted because they are liked. If you are not liked, you will not be as likely to be promoted for your efforts. Spend time getting to know the people responsible for promotions and get them to associate positivity with your name.

- **Internal colleagues:** Being kind and positive to colleagues will make work more enjoyable, and these colleagues will prioritize the work you need them to do. They'll have your back, and may do something for you they won't do for another colleague. You might even make some friends.

Overall,

-BE POSITIVE –

Successful sales is built on hard work, listening and having a good personality. No book can teach any of these things. This book can show you where to dedicate your hard work and how to win people's attention in a positive way.

GET TO KNOW PEOPLE

Anyone you work with, get to know some information about their personal lives - their families, hobbies, whatever you can that's appropriate and not related to work. Remembering this and continuing to ask about it will go a long way. People will feel attached to you, and realize you value them. This will produce better results for you.

A good way to start is to ask questions about the personal items people have on their desks or in their offices. It could be a family picture, diploma, or piece of sports memorabilia. If it's something you can relate to, start by commenting on that. Gradually build up conversation over time about these items to show interest in their lives. Don't be annoying about it, by interrupting work or asking invasive questions, but be positive and inquisitive. Soon you'll uncover common ground and the relationship will start to form.

Because you'll be friendly with your colleagues, when the time comes and you need something, they will prioritize your work. If they do a lot for you, show your appreciation in some way, like taking them to lunch or bringing lunch to them. Take care of the people in supporting roles of which you rely on for your job.

When getting to know people, make yourself a positive association. Don't be the person who wastes everyone's time.

DON'T PUKE ALL OVER A MEAL THAT HAS BEEN SERVED TO YOU ON A PLATTER

This is not literal, however don't puke in front of a customer ever. There will be times when you have a great conversation with a potential client and they will commit to giving you what you want. Albeit a request for a proposal, a suggestion to get you loaded into their system as an actual vendor, or they may even say "yes let's do this," and want to move forward with buying your services.

When this happens, make sure you understand everything you need to understand and make sure you clearly outline what will happen next on both ends. Once all of that is agreed upon, get out of there or stop talking about work unless they want to discuss more. Many times people will win what they came to win, and then they continue to talk about it over and over and in effect they have talked the client into buying the product, and then in the same conversation talk the client out of buying it.

Take note of when you get what you wanted, make sure the action items to follow are clearly established and agreed upon, make sure they have no more questions, and at that point say thank you for your time or invite them to do something social like go to lunch or get beverages. There is nothing worse then being your own worst enemy, so take note of the success and enjoy it when it happens.

ESTABLISH GOOD HABITS EARLY

I t's important to separate your work and personal life as you start out in a new career. It is important for you to establish these habits and norms early on, so they'll only get reinforced as you progress.

When traveling, prioritize your own well being over the financial savings of a company with terrible flight or hotel options. If you have personal plans that are important, don't risk missing them by scheduling a flight that gets you in an hour before the start time.

In your work life, get in a habit of giving quick and clear replies. Always do what you say you will: a staple of good sales is to under promise and over deliver. Intentionally set some expectations low so you or your product/service will really shine when it exceeds expectations. This will create a very positive emotional response from your clients, which in turn will lead them to attach themselves to you and your product or service.

Friday mornings are the best time to follow up with people or ask for something. People are usually always in great moods Friday mornings.

ADAPTING

R arely do things go as planned. Be ready to adapt when they go to shit.

You may fly somewhere specifically for a meeting, only to have it be cancelled as you land. The product you sold might not work on the launch. Do not set your mentality as "things have to go one specific way, as planned, or the world will end."

Instead, be open, flexible, and maintain a mindset of "When things go wrong, and they will, I can figure it out and find a solution, or even a better option." The saying "every challenge is an opportunity" may be corny, but it's valuable once you get your head around it.

Remember, whatever happens is most likely *not* the end of the world. When shit falls apart, remind yourself of that. Don't freak out, calm your emotions, and then find the best options. Always try to improve and work on things in your control. For things out of your control that fall apart, take a deep breath and either work with the people who can get them fixed for the future or move on.

READ MORE

The power of a well-spoken individual is underestimated. The more you know, the more you can relate to people. The wider your knowledge base is, the more interests you can connect to. As long as you aren't a condescending smart ass or pretend you know more than you do, you'll inevitably find people in the business world with similar interests to yours, or at least ones you understand. That will increase your likability factor.

Read the news. Find a magazine or two like Business Week or The Economist, or one generally related to what you do. Reading is also an excellent way to use your time when traveling for work. You clearly can read as you are reading this, so set yourself a part from others by knowing about a variety of things.

It's good to be generally current on industry news, but not essential to know absolutely every detail about it. Spend some time to broaden and enrich your knowledge base. Books on human behavior and psychology are great, because they'll help you understand humans more, and humans are the core of sales. Negotiation books are good too. Be sure to find books that are interesting to you. If a book sucks, put it down and find another.

BUSINESS MEALS

When you get a big win or sale, take the people who helped you to a meal. Get your boss's permission to expense it, in the spirit of improving relationships between the sales team and the people who support them. If your boss doesn't approve the expense, but you've made a lot of money as a result of the sale, still take the people who helped you to lunch or order lunch for them. Find a way to express your gratitude and get to know them.

When you're getting to know someone or establishing a relationship outside your organization, it's a good idea to schedule meetings right before lunch. This way you can invite them to lunch after the meeting, and get to know them.

Once a relationship has been established and you need a potential client to make a decision, talk to them first thing in the morning or right after they have eaten. Avoid asking for things from people who are working on an empty stomach. There is some tricky science here on which I'm not an expert, but first thing in the morning or right after lunch is best time to ask for a decision.

LET'S PARTY

*Don't Be The Drunkest When
Drinking is Inevitable*

I n sales, partying is inevitable and part of the culture. Expense accounts and booze go hand in hand. Navigating this doesn't have to be tough. Just keep one rule in mind: never be the drunkest one in the group. If you're drinking with a client or coworkers, always stay one drink behind them. Drink plenty of water. If someone orders shots, chances are discretely dumping yours will be better for you than taking it.

Going out together can be a lot of fun. But if the drinking gets to a point where someone in the group pisses their pants and passes out in the hotel lobby, make sure that person isn't you.

When you're getting ready to go out for a night

of fun on a work trip, set your alarm for the next day's meeting or flight before you leave for the evening. Have your clothes laid out for the next morning and pack your bag if needed. You'd be surprised how grateful you will be for these two things when the time comes.

PUT YOUR
PHONE DOWN

*Do Actual Work and Stop
Looking at Social Media*

T urn your personal phone upside down and don't aimlessly cruise the web while you're working. This only wastes your own time as a salesperson. Do you want to be at the office for 3 hours and get quality work done or 6 hours with nothing to show for it? You can scroll social media on your time off.

Dedicate work time to doing what needs to be done. When everything's accomplished for the day, you'll feel better getting out of there and exploring Instagram or whatever your social media poison is. Remember the part of the book where I said you want to work for a company that measures actual results instead of how many calls you made? If you are working for a results oriented company, you should be able to work a schedule in which the 9-5 schedule doesn't apply, as you're working the hours you need to work to get the job done. Some days that could be only a few hours!

Now, if you're using social media to sell your product or service, that's a different story. If you do it right and target the right people, it's actually a very effective way to get people to buy stuff. I'm not an expert, so I recommend learning on your own how to effectively use it if it's applicable to what you're trying to sell. This is also more of a marketing focused activity.

PERCEPTION OF OTHERS' WORK GETS IN THE WAY OF ACTUAL WORK AND CREATES STRESS

People are naturally jealous. Those who don't do sales often have a glamorous perception of the traveling life of a salesperson. From an outside point of view, salespeople get paid to travel, stay in nice hotels, go to fancy meals, and go to drinking events all on the company dime. Meanwhile, those outsiders have to work 9-5, five days a week, and often spend more time gossiping about colleagues or chatting about TV than doing compelling work.

The outsider does not see the delayed flights that make you miss an important event with loved ones. They don't feel the back pain caused by flying in coach for 6+ hours or the delay at a connecting airport because your company made you take the cheaper flight option to save some money and that delay caused you to miss the second flight which resulted in you getting home at midnight instead of 3 in the afternoon.

The outsider does not see the sleep you sacrifice to fit all your meetings in, nor the times where someone in another state will schedule a meeting with you and then decide to take a vacation without telling you about it, so you have wasted two days of your life of travel to have a meeting with someone who isn't in the office you traveled to.

The outsider, or the coworker who made a mistake which caused the problem with a client they don't work face-to-face with, but you do, doesn't have to face the wrath of the client. The coworker gets to go along their merry way, while you deal with an angry client who you might have a personal relationship with.

Jealousy from coworkers – of salary, flexible hours, and travel – is not uncommon in sales. You will have to deal with it all. Ultimately, the best way to deal with it is to always exceed your numbers, focus on yourself, and manage the perceptions of the people who have a say in your career path and opportunities within the company. Managing perceptions is addressed in the following chapter.

FIND THE
LOOPHOLE

L ife is all about finding the loophole. Learn the infrastructure of what you are working with and then find the loophole, also known as the shortest way there. It may sound ambiguous, but it won't be if you make it as simple as possible. Keep noting what works for you and what doesn't, then repeat what works. Learn the habits of the people you work with and pay attention to the details to design your own process and way of doing things. This will minimize the amount of work you have to do in the future, and can be applied to all elements of your work.

Remember: sales is measured in numbers. The higher your numbers, the better you're performing. But numbers are not everything. An unfortunate truth is that peoples' perceptions are almost as important as the numbers themselves. Managing peoples' perceptions by taking advantage of loophole elements is very important.

An easy one off the top is to announce your big wins on a big scale (see chapter *Getting Credit: Perception is Reality*). A subtler type of perception management is below, and only should be used with people who have influence over your professional opportunities within the company.

You know your boss comes in at 9, leaves at 3, and takes a 90 minute lunch around 11:30. You know this boss complains about people who come in after they do or leave before them. You know they complain about people not being available at their desks. Where's the loophole?

Shift your schedule and come in by 8:45 at the latest and leave at 3:15. Maybe even take your lunch at 11 and be back before 1, right before they will be back. As long as you're getting your work done, meeting your numbers, and don't give your boss a reason to complain about you - you are creating a perception of always being at your desk working, aka a hard worker.

Now this is one very small loophole, and I don't encourage you to focus all of your time and effort to creating these types of perceptions (especially not if your real work suffers). Just do it for the people who have a say in where your career goes in your company. Focus on getting the real numbers-based results, and take perceptions into account with how you handle yourself around the people you work with. Create a great perception, even though it might not be exactly who you are.

Another simple example is maybe you are really a party animal, but your bosses don't know that. You can keep them from ever knowing that so they only view you as the utmost professional of employees. Simply don't talk about being hung-over, or get hammered, when you're with them. Please note I am NOT encouraging you to be a functioning alcoholic, drink excessively, nor how to successfully maintain your job while drinking in excess.

There are an infinite number of loopholes you can work with. Of course, be ethical, exceed your numbers, and don't do bad shit.

HOW TO SAY "HEY DOUCHEBAG, I NEED YOU TO DO YOUR JOB" NICELY

Most times to completely sell a product, you will be dependent on other people. Those other people don't always do what they say or are supposed to. You need to let them know when it affects your output.

Always word things as kindly as possible, while including the critical information that shows you're trying to get work done, and what the impact of the work will be, but that others are hindering your process. In some very aggravating circumstances, you may enjoy saying "Hey you fuckin moron, I have seen you on your personal phone multiple times today and chit chatting around the office, so don't ignore my email or tell me you are too busy to pull the information I need," but you simply can't do that.

Instead say,

"Hi So and So, I understand you're very busy, but I really need your help. We're working on a project with a client worth (enter $$$ number here) and the process is currently suspended, as further steps rely on the information I need from you."

Make sure your facts are indisputable before you put out a message like this. Document your communications with any employee who hinders your progress with times, dates, and emails in case you need to escalate it to their boss.

When someone still isn't doing what they are supposed to, and that affects your output, you might want to tell their boss, "Hey, your shitbag employee isn't responding. I need this or we won't get the sale." But if this will land you in trouble for inappropriate work talk. Instead, use the wording and guidance below.

If you've sent multiple emails, tried to talk in person, and left one voicemail to a colleague who hasn't responded and is not on vacation, go ahead and reach out to that colleague's boss. Simply forward the multiple emails in a new email, and include any additional notes from your documented interactions (or lack thereof) with the employee, with a note like this:

"Hello (insert their name),
I hope you are having a nice week. I need your assistance please. I reached out to so-and-so, and also called them, but can't get ahold of them/they haven't been able to take care of the request. I hope everything is ok. Can you please help, as I am working on a client critical matter for some potential new business?"

Don't be the boy who cried wolf: only raise this issue when it's a real issue that you've tried to address yourself. Be prepared to have a conversation with the person's boss afterwards on how the situation can be avoided in the future. Also, do not copy the person you are talking about when sending this email to their boss.

PROBLEM SOLVING

No matter what you do, problems will arise. Instead of complaining about them, find ways to solve them. Gather information about what happened, identify a solution and way to minimize it from happening again. This is elaborated in the following chapter.

If you find yourself constantly solving problems that result from either the poor performance of your colleagues or the product/service you're selling, work with your manager to get the problems solved. If the problems do not get solved, your best option may be to look for another job.

TRUTH AND ACTION WORK BEST

Always be honest with your clients and potential clients. If you or your company has fucked up, own up to the mistake, explain why it happened, and lay out what you're doing to minimize the chances of it happening again. This formula is simple:

- Mistake happens
- Say you messed up and it is you/your company's fault
- Explain why it happened in detail
- Explain what you are doing to make up for it
- Explain what steps you have taken to minimize the chances of this mistake happening again

The simple words "I/We made a mistake' go a long way. Use them. DO NOT LIE ABOUT WHAT HAPPENED. Never underestimate peoples' ability to know what really happened or when they are being lied to. This will blow up and damage your business and credibility.

On the other hand, if you handle mistakes honestly and openly, the mistakes can be the foundation of positive business and relationship breakthroughs. People like to be included and feel like they're in the loop. If you have an open discussion with them about what happened, and how to work together to prevent it, then they feel like a partner, and your relationship will grow.

This also applies to internal colleagues. Never try to cover something up. Be open and honest, admit your mistake, and make it right.

Usually some kind of compensation to the client, like a discount on the service involved, is a huge help. Don't cheap out on this. A negligible discount is an insult when your product/service caused problems and it was your company's fault. Do as much as you can to make the situation right. If the client was financially affected as a result of the problem your company caused, work with them to make it fully right. They will appreciate it.

SPEAK THE TRUTH IN SHORT SIMPLE SENTENCES

Simple answers in simple sentences go a long way. Remember that as you talk to people.

Don't be a name dropper. Only speak of things you know and can back up. If you use a company's name and say you work with them, you had better have a name of the person you work with and a specific example of the work you did. Don't BS people to make yourself sound better than you are. They will see right through it and resent you for wasting their time.

If someone asks you a yes or no question, answer with a yes or no. Even if not everything is yes or no, only answer the actual question asked of you. If an explanation is needed make it concise.

If you ask someone a question that can be answered in a few words, and they give you a three minute dissertation, they are most likely hiding something or bull shitting you. Remember that.

To identify people who are bullshitting you, listen to for long elaborated sentences with trigger/keywords. Keywords are bullshit. The more keywords you hear or read without actual information, the more bullshit someone is trying to feed you to cover up their actual lack of knowledge.

If you talk to someone, and at any point they say,

"We want to maximize sales revenue potential by minimizing risks and alleviating the external market factors through an extensive due diligence process while gaining a better understanding for the overall market and client needs through enhanced interactions and business development while leveraging our partner relationships with high profile vendors which allow us to create a unique offering that offers a niche experience which will accelerate our growth beyond market expectations."

Then that person is going to crash and burn in

a meeting with most people when all that is required is a simple "We will use what we have available to work closely with the customer to win their business."

THROW OUT "THE SALES ALPHABET"

S tay away from the overused sales terms. The ABCs of sales one of the stupidest things you will hear (Always Be Closing) and if you have a manager tell you that, then be careful or get out. Get rid of the term "closing", douchebag.

Let's look at that one for a second. If you are always closing, then you are showing the client that you are only interested in the money. Yes, business is all about business, but if you really want that money, you have to show the client you care. You have to show them you take the time to listen and learn and make them feel good about working with you.

By listening and learning you can adapt to the client's needs. You can learn their pain points. You can develop product enhancements which will earn you more money. If you are always closing, you are going to always be annoying and distracting. Remember that the movie/play in which the ABCs of sales was made famous is about garbage people peddling garbage.

Don't be a salesperson who sells things to people they don't need nor want.

AVOIDING TRAVEL BURNOUT

*Go Somewhere Unique
and Take Care of Yourself
with Diet and Exercise*

Sales often involves a lot of traveling. This can be a perk or a drawback. A great way to enjoy it and not burn out is to get out and do something unique wherever you go.

This doesn't have to be something crazy adventurous. It could simply be a park, restaurant, or museum. Whatever it is, find something you can only do in that location and make yourself do it. Don't go to chain restaurants for every meal or stay in your hotel when you're not in meetings. That is a surefire way to get depressed and miss opportunities to see more of the world.

An expense account makes it easy to eat and drink in excess. No surprise, these effects can impact you badly in the short and long run. Make a conscience effort to eat well and moderate your drinking, so you will have more energy, feel better, and not get fat.

Exercise is key. As mentioned above, your "something unique" may simply be going for a walk. You can also hit the hotel gym, go jogging, find a yoga class in the park, or do whatever else you can outside of your room. Large hotels have big stairwells that you can go up and down for exercise. When booking a hotel, look for ones with gyms or in safe areas where you can walk outside. Ask the concierge or front desk for a walking route. These little things help a lot, especially with keeping a positive mindset around clients and potential clients.

RETAIN YOUR CLIENTS

You spent all this time getting your client, and now you want to keep them. It's easier and cheaper to retain a client than get a new one. Here are the basics of good customer service and client retention:

- Respond as quickly as possible
- Do what you say you will
- Always develop/strengthen the relationship
- Visit your clients
- Listen to what your client says about working with your product/service and make improvements based on the feedback
- Do everything you can to make sure your product works properly

This is explained more in depth in the book "Pat's

99 Cent Book on Million Dollar Customer Service".

PART 2 – STARTING A NEW SALES JOB/SALES ENDEAVOR

We'll now focus on the specific steps to take when starting a new sales endeavor. These are not universal, but most will work with the majority of corporate sales.

STARTING IN SALES

I ncluding some outlined in Part 1, here are the principles to remember from your first day of sales to your very last.

- Nothing beats great customer service
- Client relationships are critical
- Take time to learn about the clients' experiences with the product you are selling
- Do what you say you will
- Under promise and over deliver
- Show the client you care about them and their problems (at least give them reason to believe you do)
- Respond as quickly as possible

The tough truth about sales and customer service is people are more likely to remember when they receive bad service. If a product/service is delivered flawlessly to a client 100 times and something goes wrong once which causes a nightmare, that nightmare is what the client will remember. They will also explicitly remember what you did to save the ship or let it sink. People's memories are the stickiest when there's a strong emotion involved.

TRAINING FOR THE JOB

W hen working a new job or with a new product or service, focus your attention on answering the following questions to build your foundation for success:

- What is the value of the product?

- Who should I talk to to get shit done around here?

- What non-people resources are available for me to do my job?

- What are current clients' success stories?

- What's needed to deliver the product or service to the client?

- Where are the pain points the product or service solves?

These are the questions you need to make sure your trainer or manager answers. Some companies may have training programs and some may just throw you right in the job. Either way, make sure you focus on knowing these answers in and out, as they form the core of your sales abilities. Each question is explained in the following chapters.

For those of you starting a new business, take extensive notes on the responses to the above questions as you expand your business. You will use these notes to develop your own training program when you start your own sales team (addressed in book three on Advanced Sales).

WHAT IS THE
VALUE OF THE
PRODUCT?

I n other words, why do people buy the product? You need to know how the product or service being sold benefits the business or people using it. Learn the stories of the product/service as it is used by clients. Learn what they did before they had the product/service and the positive effects experienced after using it. Focus on the differences it made in clients' processes and results. Ask your boss and new colleagues to help explain this to you.

The best way to learn this is to talk directly to an existing good-standing client. Ask your boss if you can schedule a casual lunch meeting with a client, then have your boss or the account manager make an introduction: "This is our new employee and we are training them. We would like for them to hear directly from one of our best customers how our product/service has benefited them."

When a free lunch or dinner is involved, this is an easy conversation to make happen. Focus on the before and after story, as in what the client did before using the product/service and after. Listen to the words and phrases they say, because most likely other clients will use the same words and phrases. These conversations will form how you talk to new potential clients.

You can play the new employee card and ask basic questions like "How has our product helped you out?" or "What did you do before working with us?" or "What do you like about the product, and what do you not like or think could be improved?" Get to a point where you're confident answering these questions from the receiving end.

Asking a client if they think anything can be improved is a great way to create sustainable business, as long as your company uses the information you found. If they don't use it to improve, you'll be wasting everyone's time by asking. For sure, there are lazy people out there, working for companies that don't care, who will take helpful feedback from clients and then spend more time inventing excuses for why it can't be acted on than on solutions to address it.

In any case, when starting in sales, you do not need to focus on improving the product yourself. Focus on getting a good grasp on what you are doing first.

WHO WILL GET
SHIT DONE HERE
FOR ME?

When you start, ask your manager or trainer to introduce you to everyone you will work directly with. In sales, you'll likely work with people from these groups: accounting, legal, operational/product support, shipping/product distribution, product management, tech support, finance (many times a different group of people work to make payments as opposed to receive payments), and senior leadership. This list is not all encompassing as every organization is different.

Keep a record of everyone you need to talk to, what they do, and their contact information.

Meet all these people and don't be a dick (see chapter *In Other Words, Don't Be a Dick*). Make a good impression on them and start developing relationships, as described in Part 1's chapter *Get to Know People.*

Make sure you have a good understanding of what these individuals do, what you might need to ask of them, and what they need from you in order to give you what you need. Here are the starting questions to ask:

- What has your engagement process been with people in my position in the past ? / What is the ideal interaction between us, given what we both do here?

- What have people in my position asked you do to, that you can and can't do? / What are the tasks or action items I can ask from you and reasonable delivery timelines of those items?

- What can I do to make your job as easy as possible when I ask these things from you?

- Who is your back-up to work with when you're unavailable?

- Who else in this group do you recommend I work with?

- Do you have any pet peeves or frustrations related to our work together that I can try to avoid or help mitigate?

- Who do you report to?

Take notes of everything they tell you. Also be sure to introduce yourself to anyone else brought up in conversation and ask them the same questions. KEEP ALL THESE DETAILED NOTES FOR YOUR REFERENCE IN THE FUTURE. Other relevant question may arise during the conversation. Keep track of those as well.

WHAT NON-PEOPLE RESOURCES ARE AVAILABLE FOR ME TO DO MY JOB?

E very company has a pool of resources available to them. These could be a client relationship management (CRM) software like Salesforce, an internal system to file requests for technical support, an expense report system, a subscription to a news service, or a way to order more office equipment. Whatever the resources are, find out what's available and how to access them on your own.

If you're not familiar with a resource, ask to be trained on it. Take step-by-step notes on how to use it in the future, so you can avoid bothering other people or the person who showed you how to do it. A great way to annoy any person but a trainer is to ask them multiple times about a routine step they've already shown you, when you didn't take notes or try to retain the information.

Note there's a difference between asking for help on variable situations vs. asking for help on a process that has clear, defined, and routine steps. Always ask for help on variable situations when you aren't sure what to do, and discuss these with your manager. For the latter, just take the notes, learn the steps, and move on.

WHAT ARE CURRENT CLIENTS' SUCCESS STORIES?

A sk your trainer and manager to share success stories with you from current clients. Ask them for sales which were challenging and ask what the difficulties were. Ask who a few of the best clients are and what makes them the best. You may also get into this if you meet the clients directly. The success stories will become your own.

Eventually you'll be able to say "We had this one

client that was doing X before they started working with us, running into these X-related problems. And then we helped them and now they are succeeding with Y."

When you're selling to clients in the same industry or business segments, most times they all share the same or very similar challenges. When you can relay information of how your product/service helped to solve a challenge in the language and processes they're familiar with, it will help you win them over and make the sale.

If you are selling a product that can be used across multiple industries/client types, then spend time identifying the most lucrative ones and focus on them. Creating a specialization of selling to specific client types will allow you to be more successful.

WHAT'S NEEDED TO DELIVER THE PRODUCT OR SERVICE TO THE CLIENT?

You'll have to understand everything that's needed in order to deliver the product/service to the client. This is different for every company and every product/service. Here are basic questions you need to ask to get this information:

- What is the timeframe to deliver the product/service from when the client confirms they want it to the time they receive it?

- What information/documentation do I need from the client before we can deliver the product/service?

- What are the internal steps I must take for a successful delivery of the product/service?

- What should I be cautious of during the delivery of the product/service to the client?

By having the answers to these questions, you can create reasonable expectations to set for the client. You'll be prepared for the day when they tell you they want to buy what you're selling and ask what the steps are to make it happen. Here's a simplified example.

A client says to you, "Ok let's give this a shot. What needs to happen now?"

Your response will be, "I need you to sign this contract. In the meantime, please answer these questions as soon as possible, so we can start the process on our end. Once we have the contract signed and the questions answered, it will take about 5 business days to get you the product/service."

Because you now know all your internal colleagues involved in the process, you'll be able to make sure all the bases are covered in the product delivery (people will still fuck up along the way, but you can minimize this factor). You will also know all the steps needed to complete the delivery of the product/service to the client. This conversation and process will become second nature to you.

WHERE ARE THE PAIN POINTS THE PRODUCT OR SERVICE SOLVES?

First, re-read the chapter "What is The Value of the Product?" Be sure you know it well, and know what your product does well, too.

A great strategy to get people interested in what you're selling is to get them to talk about the pain points they have that are relevant to your product/service. When you get them to bring up negative feelings and then offer an exact solution, they are much more receptive to what you have to say.

Ask them about their experiences working with other vendors or any negative experiences they have had with a similar product in the past. You always want to learn about the client's experiences before you try to sell them something. People receive information through their lens of experience - meaning if they had a terrible experience with your company in the past, they most likely won't be receptive to you. Always find out what the client went through, did not like, did like, and what their ideal situation is to work with what you are offering.

When you ask people the right questions about their challenges, they'll realize you know what they're going through and ask for your help. Then it becomes their idea to work with you, instead of it being your idea. Getting people to think working with you is their idea is a great way of winning business. Here is a very broad example of what to ask, and how to find it out.

Let's say you're selling fire extinguishers that are lightweight and highly effective. You're talking to a potential client who for whatever reason has several fires to deal with every year. Their current fire extinguishers are heavier and less effective than the ones you're selling. You know, based on previous conversations with similar clients, that they don't like how heavy their extinguishers are.

Due to their inefficiencies, they require customers to buy a lot of them. These are the pain points.

Your first question would be, "How many fires a year do you have?"

Followed by, "During your last fire, was that fire extinguisher easy to carry around?"

Followed by, "How did your back feel after carrying them around?" (You're establishing a literal pain point here).

Followed by, "How effective was it?"

Followed by, "How many a year do you have to buy?"

If you ask a client about pain points you know you can resolve or mitigate, they'll be more receptive to what you have to say about the benefits of what you're selling. As they answer your questions, they may start to ask you questions about your product. This is exactly your goal: they'll be much more interested now than if you tell them the information without any context.

If the client does not ask any questions, after they've answered all of yours, you can nudge them by saying,

"You told me you went through 100 extinguishers last year. I know they cost $100 each, so you spent approximately $10,000 on those heavy extinguishers. Ours cost and weigh half of what those do. What is the current purchasing agreement you have with that vendor?"

Most times this will open a conversation about the purchasing of your product/service. It will not always be this easy. This simple example is to prove a point that you need to put pain points foremost in people's minds and then offer your solution.

Remember to let things flow naturally as well. The conversation will not be the same every time, and you'll sound insensitive and clueless if you keep following the script exactly. Just have the outline in your head and pay attention to how the client responds. Do not interrupt them when they start to open up to you sharing their experiences with the product.

People in the business world do not like being talked at. They want to do the talking. When they like you, then they want to have a real conversation. This particular conversation will get easier every time you have it.

Before you start actively selling to clients, learn as many possible pain points as you can. Once you know what they are, form them into questions. When you have a good understanding of those questions, focus on how to identify clients or prospective clients. LISTEN to what they say when you talk to them.

As you continue in the job, you'll find additional pain points you can work into your conversations with clients. Pain points are essential for winning new business and maintaining current clients. KEEP LISTENING to what they have to say about your product so they continue to work with you.

ORGANIZATION
IS KEY

When you start a new sales job/effort, in addition to the notes you take on information we've already discussed, take detailed notes on your targets and the work you've done for them. Prospect/Client notes will be the foundation of your work.

You can either create a database for these in an electronic spreadsheet, or insert them in a client relationship management (CRM) tool such as SalesForce.com. I do strongly recommend using an existing CRM tool vs. a spreadsheet, as it will help you track the key fields & action items.

Whatever you use, track these pieces of information on your prospects and clients:

- Company Name

- Company Website

- Contact Name, Phone, & Email - Have the data of all personal contacts you make at the company

- Date of Last Contact - Track the last date you reached out to or communicated with the client

- Notes/Follow Up - Keep notes of what was said in your last interaction or anything else relevant to it. This will help you remember the situation with client and identify what needs to be done to keep things moving forward, including setting possible follow up dates based on their priority rating - see below.

- Priority Rating - This should be a simple rank of 1, 2, or 3 so you can dedicate your energy to the right places and is further explained in the chapter *Priority Scale Ratings.*

You won't have all this information to start. That's okay. This tracking system gives you a framework, helps you remember key details, and makes it clear what your goals are. Getting these basics in place sets up your foundation for success. As you fill these fields in, you are building a potential client base.

Now it's time to find and fill in the information.

IDENTIFYING
TARGETS

When you start a new sales job, the best way to find out who your prospective clients are is to look at your company's current clients. You will most likely have a geographic territory and/or a client segment (meaning certain type of client such as "Airlines") to sell to. Work with your manager to prioritize your targets. A good manager will have a list of specific clients for you to pursue, or a specific list of characteristics of the client types they want you to pursue.

A good company or manager will also have resources/processes established for you to search for clients and the search process will be clearly defined.

A bad manager, on the other hand will say, "Your territory is the United States and you need to sell to all (enter company segment) in the United States."

When this is the case, the internet, professional associations, organization and prioritization will be your best friends. As long as you followed the steps in understanding the value of the product and talking to existing clients to learn success stories, you will have a good idea of what to look for.

An internet search of (insert company segment) in the United States is a basic way to start. It can bring results such as lists of your potential clients, associations they belong to, trade shows, industry publications, and other valuable information. Read through it all and note names of companies that could be potential clients.

If your employer doesn't have any information whatsoever about who buys their product/service, you need to bail as an employee. If you are, or are with, a brand new company with a new product and are not sure how to find the buyer of the product, that is addressed on a basic level in the following chapter and on an advanced level in the third book on Advanced Sales.

IDENTIFY THE TITLE(S) OF THE PEOPLE WHO MAKE THE BUYING DECISION

I dentifying people in your client companies who are responsible for actually buying your product/service is critical to success and efficiency. Most times, these people's titles will be consistent across the companies you are working with.

To find these, look at your company's existing clients and the titles of the points of contact. For example, if the point of contact title is "Director of Operations," then most likely there will be another "Director of Operations" at another potential client, or Operations Director or "Vice President of Operations" or some variant with the word "operations" (this varies with each organization).

If you're working for an established company which has been selling the product/service a long time, they will know the titles of the people responsible for buying the product. When you know these titles, set your sights on finding the names and contact information of the people who have them.

As every company, with its employee functions, is different, this may not always be straightforward. If you're not sure who really has the purchasing power, talk to any existing points of contact within current the current client list and ask them who is responsible for purchasing what you sell. Identify who uses the product within the organization and ask them who is responsible for buying it.

ASSOCIATIONS

A ssociations are a strong shortcut to getting the contact information of the people you are trying to sell to, as well as meeting them face-to-face. After you identify the positions of the people who buy what you're selling, find out what associations or professional groups they're part of, or tend to be in. Identify the top one or two and make sure they have a member directory and events to attend before you join the association yourself. Focus your energy on this. It will save you a lot of time in the long run.

There are many professional associations and professional groups focused on various industries. The easiest way to find the right ones is to ask your current clients if they are members of any or which events they attend. Your employer may also already be part of these associations. If they are, ask for access to the association directory or your own log-in credentials to the association's website.

If you don't have clients at this point, or you are your own employer, then do an internet search with the words "association" or "members" and name of your industry and or client segment group.

Spend time learning about the organization/ group/association. Learn what their acronym stands for. Reach out and ask what kind of resources they have available to members, as well as events, sponsorships, and advertising. Many professional associations will have a monthly publication, a member directory, and events throughout the year plus a major annual conference. The member directory and events are the reasons you should join. If an association doesn't have at least a member directory with contact information, it's probably shady and you want to avoid it.

Joining a professional group or association as a member can have a lot of other benefits, but the top two are those events full of people you are trying to sell to, and the member directory, which is essentially a listing of their professional contact info. So, if you identify the right associations whose members are the people/positions you're trying to sell to, you can simply go through the directory listings and reach out. Member directories will save you a tremendous amount of time.

When you start to reach out to people you can outline the commonality of being a part of the same association. Reaching out to people you don't know yet is addressed later in this book.

As for the events associations put on, to make the most of them, see the chapter *How to Handle Conferences.*

BUILD RELATIONSHIPS WITH THE ASSOCIATION'S EMPLOYEES

Develop relationships with the people who run the organizations and put everything together. They are a tremendous resource, because they're well connected and know the members. They also get invited to other events and many times can make introductions for you. Call the membership coordinator to introduce yourself and ask basic questions about what they do.

When the opportunity arises, take these people to dinner or drinks. Get to know them and make sure they know what you do. Keep getting to know them as you see them again. Develop the relationship first, then ask for their help once they recognize you by first name only.

COLLECTING CONTACT INFORMATION

If there are no professional association directories available to you, then take the job titles of your targets you learned and try finding their contact information through LinkedIn, Facebook, or general internet searches.

If you're unable to find information online, you can always call the company's general phone number and ask to speak with the [Insert Job Title]. They may not transfer you, or they may just transfer you to the relevant team. If that is the case, tell them you're trying to get ahold of the [Insert Job Title] or other leader of the group and ask them what the best way of doing that would be. They may give you the direct contact info, transfer you directly, or tell you it is not possible.

People can be reluctant to make phone transfers like this, so another strategy is to call a company and say "Hi, I am updating our client records, and we don't seem to have the name of the [Insert Job Title], could you please provide me with their name?" They may transfer you then, or you can call back the next day and ask for that person.

Make sure you are prepared to talk to this individual if they do transfer you (for guidance on the conversation see chapter, *Meeting in Person: Listen More, Talk Less*). Make sure you know the pain points and pain point questions well before you start calling people.

If you get their email address, a good way to reach out is outlined in the following chapters.

As you identify these people, enter their names and contact information into your client notes/ CRM software. Once you've established a list of targets, with specific people to reach out to, start reaching out to them!

THE EMAIL TRICK

This is no secret, but can be very effective.

If you have the name of the person you know is responsible for buying the product, but can't find their email by any of the means listed so far, you can do one more thing - search for the general email address format of the company.

Look at the company website for any email address of anyone that works there. Say you see one person's email listed as joe.smith@companyname.com. Now you know the email format is first name-dot-last name@companyname-dot-com. So if your contact's name is Phil Smith, then chances are good Phil's email is phil.smith@companyname.com.

REACHING OUT TO THE RIGHT PEOPLE - GET ATTENTION

With contact information in place, it's time to start reaching out to people. Start by thinking, "What would get my attention if I was on the receiving end of this email?" People have short attention spans and decide if they are interested or not after two sentences (if that). Never write an opening email longer than 5 sentences. What is your reaction when you open an email from someone you don't know and see a massive block of text?

Do your research on the person you're contacting.

If you find any personal information about them through an internet search or find any common points of interest, incorporate it into your initial message. (Make sure this is public information, though. Don't be a creep!)

If you can't find anything to connect on, then simply be direct and concise. There are a few scenarios to work with when reaching out to prospective new clients, which depend on how much you know about them before you reach out.

Chances are you will hear back from 5 to 10% of the people you reach out to. This is why you will keep notes on who you contacted and when, so you can follow up. People are busy and emails get buried fast, especially emails from strangers. Don't be discouraged. Be prepared and encouraged to do follow up work.

Mark the date you reached out and set a reminder to do so again in a 8-10 business days. This follow-up email is described further in the chapter *More on That: Being an Annoying Sales Person vs. a Good Sales Person.*

REACHING OUT TO A NEW CLIENT YOU HAVE LITTLE TO NO INFORMATION ABOUT

Here is a suggested first email to someone you know nothing about, except that they have the title you've identified as the buyer of the product/service:

"Hi (insert their name),

I hope you are having a nice week. I understand you work with (insert what you are trying to sell) for (insert their company's name). We work with (insert client segment/group name, such as airlines) and have been able to eliminate challenges associated with (insert product name), such as (insert a pain point or two) and been able to (insert a benefit or positive outcome).

I'd like to learn about the challenges you experience to see if we could offer any value. Please let me know if you think a conversation would be worthwhile.

Thank you,

(Insert your name and contact information)"

The only goal of this is to get a response. That's all you're focusing on for now. People have positive associations with words like "warm" and "nice", so I suggest incorporating those into your first sentence. If you have any (PUBLIC) information about your contact from an internet search, such as their love of a sports team, incorporate a quick sentence with a positive message around their personal interest.

Note the date you sent the email and set a reminder on your email or phone to follow up in 10-12 business days if you do not hear back from them.

For that follow-up, find the original email, forward it to their same email address and include the following note at the top of the email:

"Hi (insert their name)

I imagine you receive a ton of emails and may have missed mine below. Please let me know if we can talk soon."

If they don't respond to that, call two weeks later. If you get nothing, move on and rate them number 3 on your priority scale. Again, get into the priority ratings system in the chapter *Priority Scale Ratings.*

Please note this is a basic starting point email. If you do extensive research on a company, then you can grab their attention with a much more personalized message.

The more personalized the email is, showing you've done ample research on the company and/or the person, the higher the chances are of them replying. This is the benefit of doing your due diligence before reaching out.

PLAYING "THE NEW PERSON CARD"

In some cases, you can play the card of being new to the industry to introduce yourself to a group of clients. Be selective about doing this, because the first impression you give will be that of a rookie. A prospective client may be wary about working with you knowing you're brand new.

The best way to take this approach is to research the person and company you're reaching out to and send a message like the following:

"Hello So and So,

I am brand new to (insert industry name or your

company name), and am reaching out to ask for your help. I understand you and (insert their company name) are a leader in (insert industry name/the field they are in) and I want to get a better understanding of how you operate as it relates to (insert what you are selling).

I understand you are busy, but I would be grateful for any time you can spare to answer a few questions. This would help me better understand how companies like yours operate so I can work with them productively in the future.

Thank you,

(Insert your name and contact information)"

If they are willing to talk with you over the phone, set up a time for a call and follow the guidelines in the chapter *Meeting in Person: Listen More, Talk Less.*

REACHING OUT
TO A CLIENT
WHO YOU
HAVE DETAILED
INFORMATION
ABOUT

Because this book is focused on getting started in sales, the intent is to keep it basic. As you develop your career you'll learn a lot more detail about your potential clients through more research, conversations, and experiences. You'll pick up information by talking to people who work with the person you're trying to reach.

These aspects are further explained in third book of this series on advanced sales. Some of you will reach this stage early, however. For those of you who do, here is what a highly effective first email to someone you know a lot about will look like.

"Hi John,

Bill Smith, who suggested I get in touch with you, told me you are sick of how heavy your fire extinguishers are and that you almost threw your back out during the last fire. He let me know you buy more than 100 of these fire extinguishers a year.

I have worked with several others who've had similar or worse case scenarios, I think it would be beneficial for us to talk. I just helped a client reduce their yearly purchases of fire extinguishers by 50% and our fire extinguishers weigh substantially less, so the client's back was grateful too. Please let me know when you have a few minutes to talk.

Thank you,

(Insert your name)"

All the "inside information" included in the above email is the result of researching and networking. This takes time. Again, this book is about getting started and finding people to talk to. Once you find people to talk to and talk with them, you will be able to learn the detailed information that will change you from a beginning salesperson to an advanced one.

To get there, though, we need to keep focusing on the basics. We'll resume by outlining how to prioritize potential clients in the next chapter.

PRIORITY SCALE RATINGS

A priority scale rating system will help you focus your efforts in the right areas and be the most effective in your work. After you've reached out to everyone on your initial list, create prioritized action groups of clients: Groups 1, 2, and 3. More on these below.

· **Priority Group 1** is for people/companies who respond to you immediately, express a need or interest in your solution, and/or are willing to have a conversation with you, on the phone or in person.

This group also includes any targets your manager gave you. If your manager knows what they're talking about, these could be big wins for you. If your manager only thinks they know what the big wins will be, keep these clients prioritized as #1 anyway. When they don't respond to you, you'll have fast proof for your manager that these leads are dead ends, which should free you up to focus on the actual priorities.

· **Priority Group 2** is for people who respond to you and are open to conversation from time to time, though maybe not about your solution. It's also for any companies your management or you reasonably believe could be massive clients. Keep these on your radar even if no responses are received.

· **Priority Group 3** is for people/companies who don't respond at all after multiple reach outs or tell you they are very happy with the services provided by your competition. Don't scratch them out completely, because things always change. Your competition could raise their prices or reduce their service, or the person who told you "no" could move on to another position, opening an opportunity for you with a new buyer. Keep notes on your interactions and information on these potential clients, so when the window of opportunity does open, you will be prepared.

Knowing the value of your product will further help you to prioritize your potential clients. If your product is more valuable to smaller companies than larger companies, for instance, then give higher priority to those smaller ones. Note that some CRM tools will allow you to create customized groups or there will be similar options to use.

WHAT TO DO
IF NO ONE
RESPONDS

Keep track of the dates you reach out to people. I suggest send an email first, then as outlined previously send another email 10-12 business days later as a brief follow up. Keep track of the date you send the follow up email and wait 10-12 business days and give them a phone call. When you call them, if they answer, be prepared. A suggested script is:

"Hi. This is (enter your name). I work with companies like (insert their company name) to provide (insert your product). I sent you an email and haven't heard a response so I am following up now to see if we could schedule some time to talk about your use of (enter product name) or if right now is good, I would like to ask you some questions about your (insert product name)."

This script is a very rough draft and may not fit your communication style. If they say they can talk in that moment, have your pain point questions prepared. Also you may want to send one email and then call 5 business days later. The timeline above is a softer approach which allows you to reach out to as many people as possible via email first and it will surface the ones who are actually interested which allows you to focus on them as they come up. When you have to dig deeper with follow ups, it takes more time and effort (which can be very worth it).

If you don't receive a response from anyone on your list, it doesn't mean you give up here. It means you find new ways to approach people, learn more about the people you are trying to connect with, and work to find more prospects. This can be through more conferences, other clients, partner companies, publications, or social events. More can be found on this in chapter *How to Handle Conferences.* You need to make sure you have called everyone on your list 1-2 times before you scratch them or de-prioritize them.

Continue to learn about the purchasing process of the client and the durations of any existing contracts they have. They could be not responding to you for a variety of reasons. Use this as a challenge to find out more information about all of your potential clients so you can continue to create unique approaches to them that will get their attention.

HOW TO
RESPOND
WHEN THEY DO
RESPOND

When you get a response that shows interest in speaking with you, the tendency can be to read it, get excited, and then respond immediately because you're so happy you got a positive response. While you should enjoy the moment, don't respond right away. Take a few minutes to breathe, calm down, and then carefully re-read the email before you reply.

This book can't address every possible response you will receive. But some likely general messages are:

"Thanks for reaching out, I am available Friday before noon for a call."

"Thanks for reaching out, I am interested in speaking with you, give me a call when you can."

"Thank you for reaching out, we are happy with our provider now and if anything changes we will let you know."

For the first two, or any variation, find a time when you can call them. It's the sooner the better on this, so you'll be fresh in their mind. If they give you a timeframe, work that out with your own schedule and call accordingly. If they say call when you can, either call them right away if you're prepared or reply to them advising you will call them soon, then do it within 24 hours.

If they give you the timeframe to call, reply to them saying thank you and letting them know you'll call them during the time they mention. Confirm the right number to call. Usually this will be in their email signature, but if it's not and you don't have the direct line, politely ask for it.

The third response listed is basically a nice way of saying they're not interested. Send an email thanking them for their response and advise them that you frequently travel to (insert name of the city where they are based) and hope to meet them the next time you are in town. You may get lucky and they might be up for it when you do.

THE INITIAL
PHONE CALL

People are often reluctant or uneasy about first time phone calls with potential vendors, so be sure to take the lead on explaining why you reached out to them. When you call, have a positive and uplifting voice (get yourself in a good mood before you call, because emotions carry over the phone). A simple trick is to imagine you are talking to someone who makes you happy and have a smile on your face. A simple greeting, "Hi (Their Name), this is (Your Name) from (Your Company), how are you?", is a good start.

Follow with something like this: "Thank you so much for your time today. As I mentioned in my email, I work with (insert product/service name) and my job is to learn how companies use (insert product/service type) and any challenges that exist related to this to see how we can offer help to companies like yours. I wanted to talk to you to see how often you need to use (insert product/service name) and what the challenges you have had in the past."

Another suggested approach is to ask them right away how often they have a need for the product you are selling and what kind of experiences they have had. Follow with a question on who they are currently working with and what they like and don't like about it.

From here you will have to let the conversation unfold naturally. If they begin to talk to you and open up, have your pain point questions ready (see chapter *Where are The Pain Points the Product or Service Solves?*).

If you are calling for the first time and they are not expecting your call, chances are good they say they don't have time or will ask you to schedule another time with them. If they have you schedule another time, agree to it and make sure to follow up. You can also use a variation of the script in the chapter *What to Do if No One Responds*.

The person could give you a lot of information, or they could give you no information. They could tell you they never use the service, or they could tell you they use it all the time. Take notes on what they say during the conversation and what their answers are to your pain point questions. Don't feel you have to stick to a script. In fact, if you sound too scripted, they won't talk freely with you. You want them to feel comfortable and open up about their day-to-day work.

GOALS OF AN INITIAL PHONE CALL

You have three goals for this call. The first goal is to be positive and create a good first impression. The second is to learn about their experiences with activities and suppliers related to your product by finding out the answers to the pain point questions, or more about pain points you hadn't thought to ask. The third is to get a commitment to a future action, ideally a meeting in person. By getting your contact to commit to a call of action, you are getting them invested in the process of working with you. This will pay off down the road, as they'll start feeling obligated to work with you because the time spent.

Some examples of future actions are:

- Getting them to send you a quote request, with all details you need to provide them with a quote for your product/service the next time they have a need for your service. Ask them if they have a need coming up that they know about and that gives you something to work with.

- If there's an upcoming industry event you're both attending, then setting up a possible meeting there (trade shows are addressed later in this book)

- A meeting in whatever city they're based out of (if you have a travel budget/are able to travel) or if they are in the same city you can close the conversation "well it would be great to meet you sometime soon, maybe we can go to lunch or grab a coffee soon"

If they give you a good amount of information to work with, and it seems they could become a client, ask "How can I get the opportunity to work with you the next time a need for (insert product/service) arises?" You could also ask that if they have any needs for the product/service coming up, to advise you of this so you can create an offer to provide the product/service for them.

At the end of the conversation, thank them for

their time. Let them know you travel often to the city they're in and would like to meet them in person if they happen to be around. If you live in the same city, mention it would be great to meet them and maybe you could go to lunch one day.

Whatever you do, don't be forceful about meetings or requests on your first interaction. Just starting a good relationship is the priority here. Always follow up with a quick thank you email and a note about what was discussed and how you're looking forward to talking with them again.

HOW TO GET
A MEETING

This chapter is for those in sales who are able to travel to meet clients. If you don't have the resources or are otherwise unable to travel, get as much information as you can from the prospective client over the phone and email and focus on keeping the communication momentum going. Hopefully you live within driving distance from the client and can set up a lunch or coffee meeting by suggesting it at the end of the initial phone call.

If you can travel, then do it. Getting people to like you is key in sales and a great way to do that is in person. Once you've established contact with the prospect, meeting them face-to-face is key to building to the personal relationship.

As previously mentioned, let them know you're in town for other business. Most people who don't know you will not accept an in person meeting if they think you're traveling just to meet them. If they think you're casually stopping by while in the area, then this is an easier way to get them to agree. They'll feel less pressured and overwhelmed. Another option is to meet them at a conference (see chapter *How to Handle Conferences*).

If you plan to travel to meet a possible or existing client, make the most of this. Look up anyone else who is nearby or in the same city/town. If you haven't sent them the initial email outlined in the chapters on reaching out to the right people, then send it. Add the sentence "I am planning to be in (insert their city) in the coming weeks and if you are around it would be nice to meet you in person." This is a great way to get multiple client meetings on one trip.

If you have a person's contact information, but they haven't responded to your request for a meeting, call them the night before you'll be in meetings in their city. Say "Hi, I sent you an email about meeting and I am in (insert city name). I have some extra time tomorrow, and if you're available I'd like to stop by to say hello and meet you if that works for you". Many times, they'll be caught off guard and say yes. Otherwise, since you have them on the phone, you have the chance at establishing an initial connection.

TRAVELING WITHOUT CONFIRMED MEETINGS

If you have the budget, it's okay to travel places with many potential clients but no confirmed meetings, and to take a chance. If you're willing to take this risk, it can pay off. A great approach for this is what is outlined in the last paragraph of the last chapter. Call your prospect the day before or the morning of the meeting time and say "I've been trying to reach you as I'm in town and wondering if you are free at (insert time frame) so I can introduce myself to you."

As a last resort if you can't reach anyone, you can

into walk into an office and ask the front desk to speak with the person. Tell them you do not have an appointment but were in the area and wanted to say hello. Know that this will rarely succeed and could wreck your reputation before you've begun. I advise against it, but if you have nothing else, it is an option.

HOW TO HANDLE CONFERENCES

T his chapter could also be titled "How to Handle Adult Spring Breaks."

Conferences can be a blast. They can also be an extreme waste of time. This is a group of adults who all have corporate expense cards and are away from their families, and often away from their coworkers as well. Partying is abundant and so is a lack of work or productive meetings. You can enjoy this aspect, but keep in mind what you're here to achieve.

The key to conferences is identifying attendees prior to signing up. Ask the organizer of the conference for an attendee list or see if it comes with registration. You can sweet-talk your way into getting this list by saying your attendance depends on it. Many times the organizers are also sales people and just want to make the sale of getting more people to attend.

A conference or event will have a web page that lists a way to contact the organizer(s). Reach out and say "Hello, I am very interested in attending your event, as I'm looking to meet with (enter titles of positions of people you have identified as your targets). For me to get approval to attend this event, I need to show my boss an attendee list to prove it will be worthwhile for me. Can you please provide me with a confirmed attendee list or audience profile so I can use it for the conference?"

If you can identify conference attendees as people you're trying to talk to, then it is worthwhile. If the attendee list is full of people with the job titles you're targeting, then it is also worthwhile.

Start doing what you can to get these targets' contact information: this will sometimes appear on the attendee list. The best situation for you is if you can reach out ahead of time to set up a meeting at the event. Send a message like this:

"Hi [Their Name],

I just joined the (insert association name), and I see you will be attending the upcoming event. I would love to meet you as I work with a lot of (insert client type) to help them (insert benefit of what you are selling). Please let me know if you have some openings in your schedule at the event.

Thank you,

[Your name]"

As previously mentioned, if you can find information out about the person, make sure to include any commonalities you share and/or any other detailed information that will get their attention.

If you see a potential client is attending who you've already started a conversation with, this is also a great opportunity to reach out and ask if they want to meet you for a meal, coffee, or a quick talk while on-site.

When requesting a meeting at a conference, find a location that is not in the common areas of the event itself. If you meet in a common area, like lobby or the exhibit floor, you 'll most likely be interrupted, which is not what you want when building a new relationship. An example of a better area to meet would be at a table by the hotel pool, across the street at a coffee shop, or essentially somewhere greater than 300 feet from the conference area.

If the attendee list doesn't include contact information, you'll need to use the tactics mentioned earlier to find it for your targets. If you've joined this association yourself, (mentioned in chapter

Associations) you may be able to look them up in the member directory.

MEETING IN PERSON: LISTEN MORE, TALK LESS

When you've established a face-to-face meeting, whether in a person's office or at a conference poolside, your primary goals are to start establishing a personal relationship and learn about the person's business.

To repeat, YOUR MAIN FOCUS IS TO DEVELOP THE RELATIONSHIP & LEARN ABOUT THEIR BUSINESS AS IT RELATES TO WHAT YOU DO. Here are the tactics to help you accomplish both.

- Get the person to like you by being positive, smiling, and spend more time listening than talking

- Spend more time on getting to know their business than explaining yours

- Ask all the pain point questions, and have answers on how you can eliminate those pain points. If they ask you a question you can't answer, tell them you can find out and advise them later.

- Make sure they know how you can solve their pain points

- Ask who their current supplier is, what they like and do not like about what they are working with, and how that relationship was formed

- Ask them to summarize the purchasing process for the product/service you're working with. Take notes on this. This will be the basis of how you sell your product/service to them. If they mention other people involved in the process, ask if they can introduce you, so you speak with them about their needs. You also need to know who's using the service within the company, who is ultimately responsible for saying yes or no to using the product/service (if this isn't in fact the person you're meeting with), and who's responsible for the payments for the product/service.

- Create an immediate call to action in the form of them giving you information on the spot, so you can send them information in the form of an offer or to answer their questions after the meeting. You can also request they send you information after the meeting that you can take action on.

· Find out what professional organizations/associations they're a part of and what industry events they attend (see chapter *Associations*)

· Ask who they consider to be their top two competitors, and why those companies specifically are at the top of that list. If it's a niche field, this may be obvious. So if there are only a few options that you know of, ask them what about their competitors they admire.

Keep in mind that a "hard sell" turns people off fast. This means jamming your product (figuratively) down their throat. A soft sale is better. People are always more open to an idea when they think they came up with it themselves.

A great way to do this is to follow the steps we've laid out before. Have a nice conversation with the person, listen to them and their needs, address their questions, and fill in the blanks on how your product fills their need. Keep the meeting about business, but do ask some questions to get to know them as a person.

"Well, we would love the opportunity to assess your fire extinguishers for you the next time you need it, and you have our information," is a solid way to close a subtle, successful meeting. Think about it if it was you. Do you want some socially awkward douchebag barging into your office, not letting you get a word in, making it clear you guys are not going to get along, and then telling you absolutely have to buy what they are selling? Nope.

ASK YOUR QUESTION. THEN SHUT THE FUCK UP.

You learn more with your mouth shut. When interacting with your clients and potential clients, listen first and talk second.

Ask the questions you need answers to, then listen carefully and take notes. Let the clients finish what they are saying. Yes, many times you'll lead the conversation and start by telling someone why you're talking with them. To get them to let down their guard, you'll need to state your intent and ask meaningful questions about their business. As they answer you, shut the fuck up and listen.

Do not plan out the conversation in its entirety and then stick to it so strictly that you're changing the subject when they're on a roll of opening up to you. Don't ask totally unrelated questions when they are in the middle of a sentence or continuing to talk. Let the conversation flow in a natural and easy way. This builds trust and a likability factor. It also allows you to listen to their needs, including some you may not have anticipated, so you can offer them something they might actually use.

The truth is, we're all lazy and don't want to work. We, as people, want things to be easy. People want to be successful, look good, and not do much work to look good. So make this as easy as possible for your new client. Offer them ease of use, sell them on their professional lives being better or them looking better at work as a result of what you're offering them. Tap into that urge, and you have something powerful to work with.

After every meeting, create an action item for yourself and for them if possible, to keep the conversation going.

In many cases, potential clients may open up to you if you ask them how much they are currently paying for the service your competitor provides them. It is okay to ask this question. If they don't know or don't want to share, don't force it.

If you develop a relationship with them they will share this information at some point. Make sure you fully understand the fees they pay so when you make your offer, you can directly compare it to what they are paying in an honest and easy to understand manner.

ASK A FEW PERSONAL QUESTIONS

Ask personal (but not too personal) questions to get to know your prospective client to help with relationship building. If you're in the person's office, take a mental note of their personal items and ask about them. If you're in a restaurant or coffee shop, ask if it's one of their favorite spots or what they recommend you order. You can also ask them what they did the past weekend or what they'll be doing in the weekend to come. If they mention they went on vacation, ask them what they did or where they went.

When all else fails, think: tv shows, books, movies,

music, concerts, adventures, food, and family. Everyone can talk about one of these.

MIMICRY: BE A PARROT

As mentioned earlier, learning the client's language is an important way to become a part of their world. Learn the client's industry vocabulary, especially as it relates to your product's role in specific situations and problems they have. This is especially helpful when talking about the pain points of a product or service they use. It builds trust and makes them think you truly understand what is they do (even though you might really not, you've just heard this chain of words put together a few times in a few meetings you had before this one, and now you can string them together yourself and make what you have to offer relatable).

Here's an example of this at work. Say you have a service which solves problems for clients who rely on a made-up thing called a fluffy duffy. Now, say you meet with an existing client who tells you before they started using your product, that their fluffy duffy used to go haywire because of the flux intake and the carbon burn overload which caused them to be over exposed to risks that affect their clients.

What does that mean? I don't know. What I do know is that they're not the only company to have the problem of the flux intake and the carbon burn overload - and they just gave you the wording needed to succeed with other clients. Now imagine your next meeting is with a potential client who also relies on a fluffy duffy.

Your previous meeting gave you the pain points of a fluffy duffy going haywire due to the flux intake and the carbon burn overload which caused them to be over exposed to risks that affect their clients. You know you could solve these two problems with the implementation of your product. So a great opening question for this next client would be, "Does your fluffy duffy ever go haywire due to the flux intake and the carbon burn over load and cause you to be over exposed to client risks?"

Do your see what just happened there? One conversation with one client validates their pain points in their own words, as those words relate to their business and the product/service you are selling. By listening and taking note of these words, despite not quite understanding them yourself, you can use them to talk to other potential clients in their own language. This will help them trust you, and believe you know what you're talking about, or that you at least understand the frustrations they go through. Surprise, surprise, this will lead to sales.

You'll need to actually research what you're saying as soon as possible so you can answer any follow-up questions when faced with the conversation in the future.

Specifically, research how what you're offering solves the clients' problems in detail, as well as any off-shoots. You can do this by talking with your colleagues or manager, or simply by asking the clients to go into detail about the problems they have. People love to vent about their problems, and many times clients and potential clients will open up to you more outside of an office setting.

When you're meeting with people remember the general lesson in Part One's chapter *Speak The Truth in Short Simple Sentences*.

THE POST-
MEETING
FOLLOW UP

After every meeting or conversation you have, follow up within 24 hours with a thank you email. Keep this brief. You're not trying to clutter a busy person's inbox.

Thank them for their time and write a short list of your discussion points. If they requested information or particular items from you, include these in the email or give an estimated delivery date (always overestimate this so you can deliver things earlier than expected and look good).

Below is an example of a follow-up thank you email after a meeting where the topic of skiing, among work related issues, was discussed.

"Hi [Their Name]

Thank you very much for taking the time to meet me yesterday. It's always great to meet another skier and I am jealous of the trip you are taking to Vail this month.

I enjoyed learning about the projects you are working on (be specific if you can) and hope one day we can help you with our (enter your product/service). Attached is the pricing information you requested: please let me know the next time a need arises for (enter your service/product).

Have a wonderful week,

[Your name]"

A recap like this shows the person you listened to them. Having this written record from these messages also helps you remember the conversations and people, making your job easier.

If needed, take notes during the meeting, to be sure you capture all the information – in fact, this is best practice if you're just beginning to take meetings like these. Take notes with a pen and paper. People disengage when they see someone typing on a phone or tablet while they are talking to them.

MAINTAINING RELATIONSHIPS

Keep all your relationships active regardless of their priority status. This is where your notes on your last contact/interaction with people comes into play. You never know when things will change, whether within their organization, with their current contracts, or if they themselves change jobs and a new person is responsible for buying what you have to sell. Maybe the person you know who was not responsible for buying the product gets promoted and now has that decision power.

If you have a warm relationship with someone, keep it going. If it is cold, proceed with caution. As you continue talking with people and taking notes on your conversations, their priority ratings will change. There is a fine line between being annoying vs. being a good sales person, and tracking people's responses will help you find it.

MORE ON THAT: BEING AN ANNOYING SALES PERSON VS. A GOOD SALES PERSON

I t is easy to be annoying - any idiot can do it. Being tactful in how you pursue business is your challenge, especially when you're under pressure to achieve your sales numbers, and several potential clients have told you they'll work with you but they have not yet signed any contracts or commitments. The temptation to keep following up, and following up, and following up, can be intense. Don't do this. Take a step back, and observe.

Observing people's reactions is key to not annoying those people, as well as finding the right buttons to press for successful timing and interactions. Observation and listening will be your best friends as you navigate these situations.

To determine if you're being an annoying or effective sales person, observe your interactions with people, as well as their response times to your emails or calls. If they respond quickly, with positive information that gets you closer to making a sale, you are doing a good job.

If they don't respond at all or respond with minimal wording and don't answer your questions, then it's time to gear down, Big Shifter. Keep track of your interactions with these people: the date of the last communication and what the topic of conversation was. This will allow you to set reminders to reach out to them at a later date, having given them time to consider their needs and answers. Also take time to evaluate how you are communicating with them and what they respond positively to and don't.

If the relationship is dead cold, and you can tell, then keep your distance and never leave more than two voicemails in a row with no call back (make sure these are spaced out over at least a month).

If a relationship is warm, you want to feed that fire, but don't douse it with gasoline. Respond to them as a professional contact would. Make sure to respond quickly to all communications with valuable info, ask them non-work-related questions from time to time, and find common topics to open up about. This makes the conversation more enjoyable for both of you, creates trust, and gets you the business.

KEEP
FOLLOWING UP:
MAKING WARM
RELATIONSHIPS
WARMER

As your relationship develops, and your prospective client starts expressing more interest in your product, be proactive in following up in email or over the phone after conversations and meetings. You have two goals with these messages: strengthen the relationship with the person and uncover your opportunities.

To these ends, still incorporate one personal item, and ask what they are working on as it relates to what you are selling. Be very positive at the start of the message, by complimenting the person or what they have expressed interest in, to make them more receptive to the message.

Here is an example follow up email to someone who's expressed they like the Denver Broncos and have a big project coming up which may require your assistance.

"Hi [Their Name],

I hope you're having a nice week. I saw the Broncos had a big win this weekend so I wanted to say Go Broncos!

How are things coming along with the project you mentioned when we last spoke? Is there any information I can provide you related to the (insert your product/service) needed for your project?

Thank you,

[Your Name]"

You can also choose to do a phone call instead, using basically the same wording.

Phone Rings

Client: Hello?

You: Hi (their name), this is (name). How are ya?

Client: Good.

You: Congrats on the Broncos win!

Client: Yeah! It was a great game!

You: Hey, I wanted to follow up with you on the project you mentioned when we last spoke. What's the latest update on that?

At this point, they either have an update for you or they don't. If they don't, ask them if there are any other projects they are working on related to what you're selling, and if nothing is mentioned then gracefully end the conversation. As always, don't follow the script to the letter: let the conversation flow naturally. Write down your notes on the information shared and mark a date to follow up with them, depending on what they tell you.

Whatever projects they do have going on related to what you're selling, ask what their plan is for the element you're offering. Take notes. Unless they are dead set on using another supplier, asking these questions will open the door to your opportunities, and you're one step closer to turning your relationship into a sale.

DEVELOPING THE RELATIONSHIP THROUGH MEALS AND ENTERTAINMENT

Another way to get closer to a sale is through building the relationship on the personal side outside of the office.

Spending time with someone outside their office will loosen them up. They'll share more information with you. This is why entertainment is often crucial to winning new business. If you have a good initial meeting (or second, fourth, or fifth one), suggest you go for lunch or dinner, or if the timing is right, for drinks. This is a fantastic way to develop a relationship. It also has its risks.

Entertaining clients and prospective clients can be fun and productive bonding experience. It can also go overboard. Your personal well being can be damaged by late nights, lots of drinks, and too much delicious, fancy, company-subsidized food. You can make new friends this way, but time here is also time away from people you already know and love. So, like all things, manage this in moderation.

But when you are out with a person, spend that time getting to know them on a personal level.

Think about this. When you're out of the office, do you want to talk about work or literally anything else? Most people want to talk about non-work related things at lunch or dinner, and many would rather not be at the office at all. So try to get your potential clients out.

Invite them out for lunch if you meet with them during the day. Ask if they want to have a dinner meeting if you've already met once or are at the same event/conference. The beauty of this is by getting them to talk about things not related to work, they will relax and then be more willing to talk to you about work related matters later.

There's a strong belief that taking people to meals or events creates a sense of obligation. Time away from the office doing fun things does help form a relationship and gets people to start to feel like they know and trust you more. Once you've established a relationship with a strong potential client, if you have the budget for it, invite them to an event such as a concert or sporting event (something you'll both enjoy, based on what you know about them, and make sure your company guidelines allow for this).

Make it fun for them to spend time with you. As mentioned earlier, the wild thing about not talking about work in social settings is that it will lead to more talks about work that will benefit you.

GENERAL TIMELINES FOR FOLLOWING UP

The timeline for following up, regardless of your relationship status (so to speak) is highly variable and subjective. But these general guidelines can help you gage time frames to reach out or follow up with all the people you've established contact with. Like your initial reach outs, keep these short and sweet.

- If the person is waiting on information from you, or you're working with them on an active sale (active sale = they told you they want your product and are moving forward with a commitment to buy it from you), always reply and get them what they need as soon as humanly possible.

- If the person's expressed an interest in working with you, or you've met and started establishing a good relationship, follow up every 30 days or whenever something relevant arises. Examples of relevant items are: an article or current event directly related to a conversation you had with them, a major update to your business, or letting them know you are going to be at the same event and you would like to see them. For this category, alternate your method of reaching out between email and phone calls.

- For people who have established an interest in what you have to offer, but who you haven't met: make sure to answer their explicit questions as soon as possible. Beyond that, a good time frame is to reach out every 30-40 days. For the first two follow ups, it's best to reach out via email unless you had a fantastic and memorable conversation with them over the phone. An email chain helps people remember who you are and avoids an awkward follow up conversation on the phone. Now, if they don't respond to your follow up email, wait a week and follow up with a phone call. Refer to your email as a reminder.

- For people you've met who advised they currently have no need or interest in your product, wait at least 45 days before reaching out again.

An exception is if there's an upcoming event you're both going to. In that case, ask if they'd like to have a beverage with you or just meet briefly in person so you can put a friendly face to the name

- For any people of interest who send any communications to you: respond as fast as possible. This is the best way to improve any relationship.

RESPOND
AS FAST AS
POSSIBLE

T his rule bears repeating.

Whenever you are working (as in not on vacation), respond to every email from someone you consider to be a potential client or existing client within 12 business hours. If you don't have the answer they need tell them you're working on it and then forward the email to the person internally who can give you the answer.

12 hours is a general rule because there will always be clients who are overly demanding, unreasonable, or just plain assholes. If you respond too rapidly to them all the time, they'll expect it, and if you slow down on even one response they'll get

angry you didn't answer sooner. With these clients, teaching them acceptable behavior through communication will make your life easier.

Another good way to deal with these clients is, whenever you do respond, include all of the answers they asked for, plus any answers prepared for questions they haven't asked yet or you know they're likely to ask as a result of the email.

GETTING CLOSER TO THE ACTUAL SALE

You will know you are getting close when a potential client starts asking more questions or asks you for proposals. Always make sure your communications are as clear as possible and when you present your pricing or proposal, ensure the client understands everything being presented to them. Communicate it in as few words as possible.

If you have to explain multiple parts of your offer that are common in your communications to potential clients, create a Frequently Asked Questions PDF document you can attach to the email. You want to be short, sweet, to the point, and cover all important elements. Make sure the client understands all elements that will be incorporated into any final invoices that could arise out of them using your services. If there are any important timelines, make sure to address these as well in the presentation of your services.

If you create a PDF with information, spend some time to make it look nice and official. Remember people like pictures and do not like reading lots of text. If you have a marketing team, ask them if they can assist or have any templates. If you don't have a marketing team, do what you can with your word processor. Clients always like seeing their logo on things, so if you create something specific to them, put their logo on top and include some note like "Specially Prepared for (insert their name)."

Send your proposal and either call them the next day to confirm they received it and ask if they have any questions. You can casually ask them when they expect to make a decision and take note of what they say and that is when you follow up again. At that point or sooner they will tell you if you won the business or not. If you do not win the business, ask them why and if there was anything you could have done differently and then take notes on what they say and incorporate it into future offers if you can.

WHEN THEY'RE GOING TO BUY FROM YOU

When you've put in the work, made contacts, and established and nurtured relationships with potential clients, eventually people will start telling you they're going to buy your product/service. Many times this will come in the form of an email or phone call.

This is a great moment, however do not celebrate. Take a deep breath and immediately engage everyone at your company you need to successfully deliver the product. Double check any timelines that need to be incorporated and make sure anyone that needs to be involved will be involved and available.

As long as you followed the steps earlier, you should already have that outline prepared. Check in with everyone, make sure everything is in place and then get the job done and the product delivered.

Reply to the client thanking them for choosing you and advising them of all information/contracts etc... that will be needed to move forward and get the wheels moving on your end to deliver the product like you said it would be.

Be involved and make sure the client gets what you told them they would get. By being involved you will learn a lot about your product and its delivery which will help you in future sales and communications with clients as you can identify issues before the arise after you have been through a few product/service deliveries.

At this point you either hand the client over to an account management team or will continue to work with the client directly. If an account management team takes over, you want that transition to be as smooth as possible for the client and put the account management team in place to succeed by giving them a good introduction.

If you continue to work with the client, then you want to work on strengthening the relationship through phone calls and in-person meetings and events as outlined in this book so they start to advise you of potential business instead of you having to call them.

A good move no matter what is to call the client after the product has been delivered and ask them how everything went. Before you make the call, talk with everyone who was involved internally to make sure there were no issues. If there were, then find out why they happened so you can be prepared to talk to the client and advise them how the issues will be avoided in the future (if possible). If issues did arise, see Part One's chapter *Truth and Action Work Best.*

BRINGING IN
THE MONEY

The sale is ALMOST complete when the money is in the bank. Make this step as easy as possible for your clients and also for your internal colleagues. Prior to the sale of your product/service, identify the key people in the payments and approvals process on the client's side.

Know who is responsible for managing and approving your client's invoices, and who's responsible for making the actual payment. Spend time communicating with these people so they all understand your invoices, the items on the invoice, and where to send the money.

As much as you can, make the process of paying your company simple. It is embarrassing to lose a client over payment matters because you can't get your shit together and give them a way to actually hand over the money.

You want to identify the clients preferred payment methods and have those easily and clearly outlined for them. If you have your own business, it is always a good idea to accept as many forms of payment as possible.

A COMPLETED SALE

A sale is complete when the product is delivered, your company gets paid, and the client is happy.

This is simple if you make it simple, and hard if you make it hard. You need to follow the steps outlined in the previous sections, and identify everyone involved in the sales process and product delivery, as well as their managers. If your colleagues fuck this up, you'll be positioned to overcome their mistakes.

If a colleague is truly not pulling their weight, and you need to pull the rip cord and go to their boss to get it done (see chapter *How to Say "Hey Douche Bag, I Need You to Do Your Job*), do it nicely. Don't be the boy who cried wolf: only take this step when absolutely necessary and make sure your facts are solid.

Celebrate once you know the client is happy and the money, in full, is in the bank. Client happiness is key because it leads to more business from them, as well as their possibly referring your company to others. Also, if any of their employees involved in the process leave and join a competitor (i.e. other potential client of yours), you will have future opportunities there as well.

So, make it as easy as possible for them to both work with you and pay you. Make the client feel special without patronizing them. Do what you say you will do, and what they request, in a timely and professional manner.

GETTING CREDIT: PERCEPTION IS REALITY

You made a sale! Now what?

It's messed up but true: many people get by because they create an image of being very busy or doing a lot of great things. They often get away with this, because others rarely check facts if these people are doing the basics. You're truly doing great things, so take advantage of the "Perception is Reality" principle and make your accomplishments known.

The next time you do something great (complete a big sale, win a big contract), make sure the key people who are responsible for promotions know about it. These are usually Vice Presidents and

Directors of your division or the company. Look at the organization chart and everyone that has a line connecting to you that is above you is who should be on the email. Send an email to them, keeping it brief and thanking everyone involved. Here's a copy and paste template you can use:

SUBJ: Good News Email

"Hi All,

It's not every day we get to send out a good news email, so I want everyone to know that we won the (insert name of business) and we expect to make (insert dollar amount). I want to thank (insert everyone who helped you) for their hard work.

Thank you and I look forward to sending another one of these soon,

(Your name)"

Copy everyone who was involved – giving others their due credit keeps everyone happy and most times means they'll do the same for you – but make sure the email is addressed to the bosses.

VACATION PLANNING

After you've been making sales for a while, you'll need vacations and breaks.

Before you take one, identify every single ongoing opportunity you have that could come to fruition while you're unavailable. Then work with your colleagues (like those you just gave due credit to) and give them a very detailed outline of exactly what needs to happen.

If you absolutely know something will come up, advise the client involved that you'll be out of the office and unavailable. Over phone or email, introduce them to the colleague who'll be assisting them, and go through exactly what will need to be done.

Whenever you're unavailable and need your colleagues to do work for you, go over the outlines of the work they need to do and be sure they understand it. This benefits you in two ways. First, you won't be bothered while you are away and the job will get done right. Second, your colleagues will not mind helping you out when you're gone, because you were thoughtful and gave them what they needed to do it right.

BUILDING AND EXPANDING YOUR PORTFOLIO

The "80/20 rule", some common wisdom further addressed in Book 3, states that 80% of your business comes from 20% of your clients. When you are starting out, you need to focus on the items listed below in order to get to the point where you focus your efforts on targets who'll yield that majority of business to you.

- Learn the product value
- Identify your clients
- Establish relationships

- Prioritize your clients
- Ensure smooth delivery of what you sell

As you get a grasp on those, incorporate a focus on building your portfolio. Building a portfolio of clients based on geographical regions can be beneficial for reasons of convenience and cost savings.

When you exceed your goals, you will have established a good portfolio. If you have a renewable product, and you're consistently beating your numbers with your portfolio, then it's time to talk to your manager about a promotion and you use your statistics/proven results as the foundation of getting the promotion. If they don't give it to you, then start looking for another job. Never ask for a promotion without proven results which show you are exceeding what you were expected to do.

If they tell you to grow the business more with no promotion, advise them you need someone (like an account manager or sales assistant) to help you maintain the business of your current portfolio so you can pursue new business without losing the old. It's easy to get distracted from new clients by current client issues. If they don't provide you with the support you need to grow the business, look for a new job.

FREEING UP YOUR FUTURE TIME AFTER YOU HAVE AN ESTABLISHED PORTFOLIO

A person can only manage so much. That said, if you are a truly great sales person you will want to keep selling to new clients and your management should encourage that. When this happens, you need to have a support team on your current portfolio. If you're happy with your portfolio and don't want to expand, that is account management.

Work with your manager to establish the best plan. But if you want to continue growing, you'll need to hand off your portfolio to an account manager. This person should be put in place by your management, with your assistance in selecting who would be the best fit. Then you can move on as you will have more time to work on new business.

At this point, it's possible you yourself could become a manager of the person responsible for the portfolio you built. If this is the case and/or you are looking to expand beyond the basic territory you have then I recommend the next book in the series. If not, keep selling, and grow.

THIS IS THE END
OF THE BOOK

If this was helpful for you, please let me know! You can contact me through instagram @bizdevpat or at my website www.bizdevpat.com through the contact section.

If you continue to achieve success in sales and grow then I recommend Book 3 in the series on advanced sales. That book addresses international sales, building a sustainable sales team, selling to international governments, finding a market, as well as additional strategies which are more useful once you have the basics in this book established.

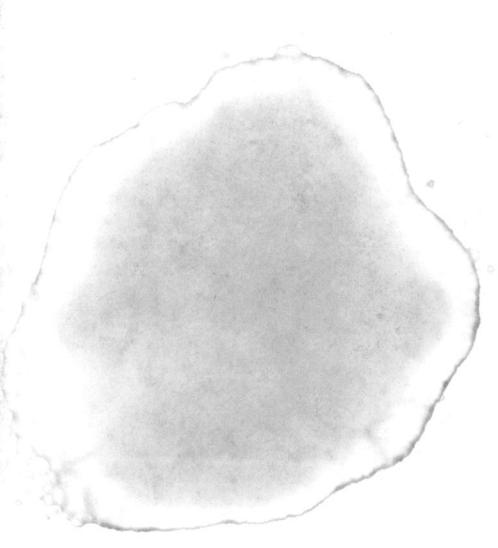

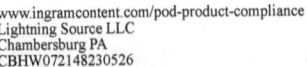